Instagram Marketing Simplified

for Contractors

How to Easily Market Your Company on Instagram without Wasting Time or Money

Martin Holsinger

Publisher: Protractor Media

Copyright: © 2018 by Martin Holsinger

All Rights Reserved

Printed in The United States of America

ISBN: 9781729338032

Cover Design and Interior Design: Rayna Bauman

Dedication
To the incredibly talented and passionate community of contracting professionals trying to build a real business while doing the craft they love.

Goal
Provide simple and practical help for every builder, remodeler, or other contractor who is passionate about their craft, but needs simple and easy help with marketing their business on Instagram.

CONTENTS

Introduction — Page 5

Chapter 1 — Page 9

Chapter 2 — Page 15

Chapter 3 — Page 25

Chapter 4 — Page 35

Chapter 5 — Page 45

Chapter 6 — Page 55

Bonus — Page 67

INTRODUCTION

Why I Wrote This Booklet

The idea for this little book came about after I wrote a few articles for the Fine Homebuilding Blog about Instagram marketing. I began to think about all the books written on Instagram marketing—most are lengthy, full of way too much information, and few apply to contractors specifically.

I wanted to compile a small booklet to help you market your business—one that would include only the most useful information so that it could be easy to read without wasting too much time on unnecessary information.

My vision for this little booklet is that it would be a helpful resource specifically applying to contractors working in the field, seeking to grow their businesses with Instagram as a marketing tool.

I do not claim to be an expert on Instagram marketing, however over the past couple of years as I've interviewed dozens of contractors for my Protractor Podcast, one thing I always love to ask a guest on the show is how he or she uses Instagram for their business. Because of all that knowledge I've picked up through interviewing, I've been able to learn quite a bit about what the best practices for contractors are today on Instagram.

I wrote this booklet because I want there to be a quick way to help contractors with their Instagram marketing; that's my intention for this booklet—something easy to read and easy to implement. Information that doesn't take too much of your time but makes a big impact on the marketing of your business.

How to Use This Booklet

My vision for this booklet is that it would *go* with you, stay with you, and be something that you come back to often. This booklet is small enough that you can carry it in your glove box to read when you're out and about; you can stash it in your desk drawer and read it when you finish writing up an estimate. You can pick it up at any time, flip just about anywhere throughout the book, read a paragraph or two and have a tip, insight, or inspiration.

I want this booklet to inspire you, motivate you, and nudge you in the right direction to help advance your marketing on Instagram.

Share the Vision

Finally, I would like to see you get a copy for each of the members of your team and have them read it. Then you can come together and talk about it corporately. Everyone may have a little different angle or insight into how to use Instagram as a company, but I believe that the power is exponential that way. Also, I would love to see you take these booklets to hand out to your friends to help them with their businesses as well.

In a nutshell, my vision for this booklet is that it would be full of actionable and useful information that's quick and easy to read—something that you come back to often and use over and over to help grow your business using the Instagram marketing platform.

CHAPTER 1

Introducing Instagram for Contractors

Ah, social media. It seems to be the raging success of our current day, attracting millions of users, and consequently inspiring businesses to "get where the people" are by creating their own accounts. If your desire as a contractor is to reach your target audience online, Instagram is one way to do that very effectively.

What is Instagram?

Instagram was developed in 2010 as a **photo sharing platform**. At its simplest, it's a place to display gorgeous pictures in perfectly symmetrical squares. Easy to use, the platform was revolutionary for online photo sharing.

Previously, sharing photos online required special access and/or a membership of some kind. You could upload your photos to a web album, but to share them with friends/family it required a direct invitation or link. Instagram has private account options, where only your 'followers' can see your photos, but with a generic Instagram account, your photos are available to the whole world!

While it was initially designed for simple photo sharing, Instagram's platform has expanded and developed over the years to include its own search engine, geo tags, video sharing, stories, etc.

From the very beginning Instagram was widely popular, bringing in a million users almost immediately. Today, Instagram has 800 million monthly users, and 500 million who use the app daily!

How Should You Use Instagram?

There are so many ways to use Instagram. You can use your account to share private and personal photos of your daily life; with Instagram's worldwide platform, you can use the platform to make a GLOBAL reach; or with location tags and network connections, you can utilize Instagram to target a niche audience such as Homeowners in Your Region.

Keep in mind that Instagram was built first and foremost as a photo sharing platform. If you're thinking of using Instagram as a place to feature your contracting business and get leads from your specific locality, you will be approaching the platform at a different angle than, say, a global influencer. As a global influencer, you would be focused on building a world-wide customer base and attracting millions of followers. As a contractor looking for a more *local* reach, you'll run your Instagram account with a slightly modified targeting approach.

It's important to develop the fundamentals of your online presence first, such as a business website that you own and control. Establish local SEO, reviews, and a quality reputation, and then use social media to drive back to your home base, your website. While Instagram is a hot platform with the ability to get good leads right now, keep in mind that it could quickly change. Establish your online presence and use Instagram as *one part* of that strategy!

How to Position Yourself

Who do you want to be on Instagram? Think about positioning yourself. Who do you want to be? Maybe you want to be THE go-to contractor in your town.

Let's say for a second that you specialize in exterior remodeling in Boston. If that's the case, you want to present yourself as the Exterior Remodeling Expert in Boston. Or maybe you're a boutique home builder that is extremely high end in a special way. You'll want to position yourself in the minds of people needing that service in your town. Decide who you're reaching out to and develop your strategy and position off that information.

One of the things that successful contractors have done on Instagram, is that they've made a conscious decision to be *all in*. You must commit to Instagram, because it takes a lot of work to grow your following and a dedicated audience. Not only do you have to post good pictures, but you'll be busy liking other people's photos and engaging with other contractors by commenting and sharing. If you really want Instagram to work for you, you must be all in.

CHAPTER 2

Getting Started

So, we've talked about mental game, determining who you're going to target in your hometown and how to position yourself. Now let's talk a little bit about creating your business profile on Instagram.

Create a Business Profile Account

Unless you plan on sharing personal life on your Instagram, you should create your account with a Business Profile. Choose the business profile option as you set up your account. This lets you share your location as well as providing you with more insights into how your account is doing with its reach.

Make It Public

I've seen some contractors on Instagram who keep their accounts private. In other words, if I'm looking at them I can't see any of their pictures unless I first send them a friend request. This doesn't make sense. If you're a contractor and you want your work to be seen, make your account public. This way, anyone can see your photos.

Choose Your Profile Picture

It's important to have a profile picture that really stands out. You want people to be scrolling through their feed and see that little circle icon with your picture JUMP OUT. You want people to know who are and to develop a positive impression as they continue to come across your account.

What TO DO:

- If *you* are the brand, you can put a professional photo of your face as the profile picture.

- If your *company* is the brand, put a high-quality image of your logo as the profile picture. If need be, get a designer to rearrange the key elements of your logo so they fit nicely in the circular icon.

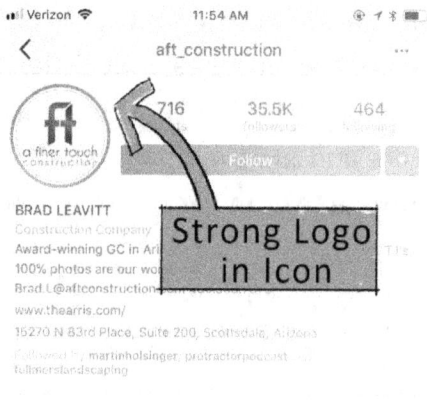

What NOT to DO:

- Do not use a picture of your business card as your profile picture.

- Do not use a zoomed out, hard to see picture of your shop or van.

- Do not try to fit a rectangle logo into the circular icon.

These little changes truly make a difference in how Instagram users will view your account. Even if you're new to social media, you want to appear as professional and trustworthy as possible!

Write a Business Description

In the space provided, write a clear, concise description of your company and your services. Make it short, yet comprehensive. Something people can read in a split second. While it may be only a few words long, put in thought as to how it will appear to your target audience. It's not the place to be clever or humorous which can too easily come off as unprofessional.

Give a Clear Call-to-Action

Include your contact information, your phone number, and email address in the description, so that your potential clients will be able to reach you immediately.

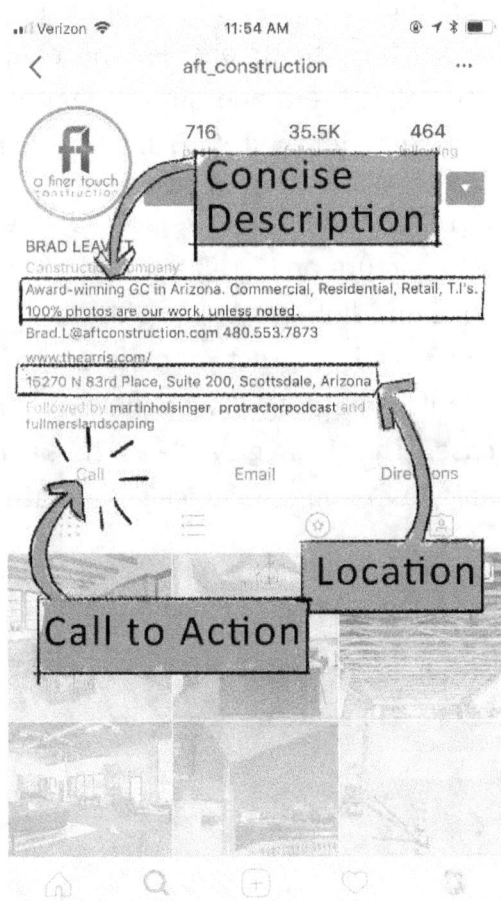

Link to Your Website

Instagram gives you the opportunity in your profile to put a Web site link. Why would you not use it? Take your followers exactly where you want them to go. If that's your blog, link it in your profile and direct them there. If it's a specific landing page you have one set up just for people who come from Instagram, link it there and direct them to it. I've seen contractors put their YouTube link there, etc.

Another great option; if you've posted a new blog post, post a picture on IG related to the blog post, and change the link in your profile to that new blog. In your caption, direct your viewers to the link in your profile, and that will take them right to your home base. This is a great way to keep your website as your online presence's foundation.

(all photos from A Finer Touch's fantastic Instagram profile. @aft_construction)

Post High-Quality Photos

Finally, after creating your profile, post pictures. It's very important for the photos to be high quality, as that will imply that your work is high quality as well. A high-quality photo of high-quality work will really jump out at a potential client.

If you don't feel comfortable taking the photos yourself, it's a worthy investment in your marketing scheme to hire someone to take them for you! Consistency in quality, where every post is perfect in and of itself will go a long way toward developing your professional, trustworthy online reputation.

CHAPTER 3

All About Hashtags

Posting high quality photos of your finished work on Instagram is just the first step towards making the app work for you and your business.

Using Instagram's hashtag feature is an easy way to promote your contracting business within the app, increase views on your posts, and create an online community.

How Do Hashtags Work?

Instagram hashtags work within the app both as a search engine and a catalogue. Searching for specific hashtags within Instagram is the easiest way to find a localized and/or specific post. Searching for a hashtag on Instagram will show you all the posts on the app that contain that keyword. Hashtags look like this:

#contracting #marketing #homeremodel #hashtag

Generally, hashtags are placed in the caption or description of a photo; you can use up to 30 hashtags in one post.

Why Should I Use Hashtags?

Imagine a homeowner living downtown in Seattle, Washington. They're looking for a contractor to do their kitchen remodel, or redesign their mudroom, or put a pool in their backyard. They open Instagram and search #kitchenremodel, #mudroom, and #backyard #pool. Instagram shows them all the pictures that have been hashtagged with those keywords.

You can have the most gorgeous, high-quality photo of a backyard pool posted on your timeline, but if you don't tag your pictures with the proper hash tags, Instagram will not know to provide your relevant photo to the homeowner.

It's been proven that Instagram posts with hashtags get much more interaction within the app than posts without hashtags. Without hashtags, it's easy for your posts to be seen once and then lost in the algorithm.

Here are five tips for optimizing hashtags on your contracting Instagram account. Following these tips will help you get your posts into more Instagram users' view, so you can provide value to more people.

Choose Relevant Hashtags

Each time you post a photo, think about what hashtags correctly represent your post. For instance, if you did a kitchen remodel in Scottsdale, Arizona, here's a list of hashtags that would be applicable to your post highlighting your work.

#generalcontractor #kitchen #kitchenremodel #remodel #kitchendesign #indoordesign

You should also include location tags so that local Instagram users can find your post when searching for a kitchen remodel.

#Scottsdale #Arizona #Arizonaremodel #Scottsdaleremodel

Remember you can use up to 30 hashtags per post! Use those tags to tell Instagram who you are, what you do, and where you are from. Local users can find you if they're looking for someone to hire, and non-local users can view your photos as inspiration within the hashtag searched.

Diversify Your Hashtags

Instagram also tells you how many people have used each hash tag. When you enter in a hash tag such as #kitchen remodel, Instagram will show you how many times that hashtag has been used. It's difficult for your post to be found in the tags that have millions of posts, so use a mixture of hash tags. Choose some that have less posts and a few more popular ones. Use hashtags like #design, #remodel with tons of posts, but also include specific tags such as

#Seattlelandscapingdesign.

#seatthehomeremodel

This helps boost your post both in the most popular search results and the more niche results.

Create a Custom Hashtag

Instagram's hashtags can easily be used to create a portfolio of your own work, by making a hashtag unique to your company. This could be just **#yourcompanyname**, or something else that's clever—any hashtag not taken by another company. Use this hashtag on all your posts. If homeowners and satisfied customers want to post pictures of your work, ask them to tag it as well.

Use your custom hashtag to develop a community centered around your work, providing value to anyone who searches your hashtag. People will begin to recognize and identify it with your company, and Instagram users can search your custom hashtag to see the complete collection of your work within the app.

Tag Team

You should also use hashtags as an opportunity to collaborate with strategic partners. A strategic partner is someone you work with in your local area that doesn't directly compete with what you do. For instance, if you're a custom builder, maybe it's a local designer. Or if you're a general contractor—a plumber or landscaper.

Determine those people who are your strategic partners, the ones who all target the same community, work with your same residential contracting market, but are not directly competing for the same job. Help them out by tagging them in your posts (by typing @theirusername) or use *their* custom hashtag.

They will see that and can reciprocate for you! You can help each other build a strong online collection of supportive services.

Follow Hashtags

Instagram recently released a new feature where you can follow individual hashtags. If you choose to follow a hashtag such as **#bathroomremodel**, each time a photo is posted with that hashtag it will appear in your feed.

Following relevant hashtags is a good way to stay up-to-date with what's happening real time in the contracting world. You can also encourage your followers on Instagram to not only follow your account, but also to follow your custom hashtag to see other photos of your finished projects.

Summary Thoughts on Hashtags

The photos that you choose to post on your company's Instagram account are important—there is no question about it. High quality photos of your finished work are the foundation of your Instagram marketing efforts; what could be more inspiring to a potential customer than a job well done?

However, getting these photos into the eyes of Instagram users in your locality without using hashtags is difficult. Using hashtags adds additional value to your posts by making them searchable, relevant, and ultimately easy-to-find for your potential customers.

CHAPTER 4

Optimizing Instagram Stories for Contractors

If you've taken your business to social media, you're not alone. More and more companies are creating social media accounts to develop online connections with potential customers. Instagram is the perfect social media platform for a contracting company wanting to create an online following, a streamlined portfolio, and quality customer connections.

Today we're going to look at Instagram Stories, why you should use them, and a couple ways to make the most of this special feature.

After its release in 2010, Instagram existed almost exclusively as a photo-sharing app. It was a place to share square-cropped pictures with your followers. In 2016, Instagram released a new feature...Stories. Instagram stories are pictures and videos that, once posted, disappear after 24 hours.

I'll be honest, I was a bit nervous when Instagram stories first came out, but since then I've seen the opportunity stories give you to show your potential customers the behind the scenes of your business.

So, WHY Instagram Stories? What's special about them? Here are three reasons you should use Instagram Stories on your contracting social media account.

Why Instagram Stories are Awesome:

1. They're Easy

Posting an Instagram Story is quick and simple. You open the app, swipe to the right to open the camera, take the picture or video, and post it to your story. If you want your followers to see a special moment in your day but don't have time to take, edit, caption, and post a photo, Instagram Stories are perfect. Take the video, maybe write some quick text with the four different font options and post! Voila!

2. They're Authentic

Instagram stories give you a chance to show your followers your genuine self and company. It's a real, unedited presentation. Stories are different from your normal Instagram posts; they're generally less polished and more spontaneous. They're a fantastic way to show your followers your day-to-day life and the Man/Woman Behind the Business. When your potential customers are let into your personal story—your projects, behind the scenes, etc.—a connection is built from that authenticity.

Ask your followers questions! If they reply to your story in a direct message, be sure to respond as soon as possible!

3. They Offer Diversity

How do you post project updates and behind-the-scenes photos and videos without messing up your curated, high quality Instagram profile? Stories! Posting the less glamorous daily milestones on an Instagram Story lets you share temporary, personal information with your followers while still maintaining your professional profile.

How to use Instagram Stories to Provide Value to Your Followers

Here are a few ways to use Instagram Stories to reach and provide value to your potential customers on social media.

If you've already created an Instagram account for your contracting business, give Instagram stories a try. Your followers will appreciate the personal connection and authenticity this feature provides them.

Teach People

Use Instagram stories to show DIY projects. Take your followers on a step by step process of building porch steps or installing kitchen cabinets. Get on your stories and show by example how you fit that crown mold or how you lay pavers.

Whatever it is that you do well, you have the ability to teach other people how to do it. Instagram Stories are good way to do that. They're easy to watch and the genuine connection is awesome for project-oriented posts like that.

Show Behind the Scenes

What's more intriguing than seeing a gorgeous photo of a home remodel? Seeing the behind the scenes of what it took to make that remodel happen!

Instagram stories are such a good way to bring your potential customers into the sometimes-messy, but always rewarding process of building something from the ground up.

Advertise Your Business

Instagram Stories are a clever way to promote your contracting company on social media. For one thing, they're featured at the top of the Instagram app's page; your followers will see them before they see the other posts below.

Do some teaching, showing behind the scenes of what you're doing, and then every now and then throw in an advertisement that takes tells people to take action. Don't post an ad every single time, or people will start just swiping through your stories and not watching them every time they show up. Make your Instagram Story ads short; make them sweet; make them pop.

CHAPTER 5

Tools and Apps to Optimize Instagram Stories

While Instagram contains nearly everything you need to direct your company's IG marketing scheme from within the app itself, sometimes it's helpful to pull from other resources for your posts and stories.

Here are a few apps and tools I've found and seen other contractors using that will help you create and tell awesome Instagram stories.

Polls:

Instagram Stories offer a feature within the story—a poll. Simply ask your followers a question, i.e. "Which color of hardwood floor should I lay in this kitchen?" Post pictures or videos of both options and then create a poll with the two choices. While tapping through Instagram Stories, polls are almost impossible to resist. This is an excellent way to engage your followers and make them feel like they are a part of you and your company.

Storeo:

Currently, Instagram Stories only allow video up to 15 seconds long. This can make posting a long video complicated, as you either must pause talking to restart the video or slice a previously-shot video into short segments and upload it separately.

Storeo is the #1 iOS app for making Instagram Stories longer than 15 seconds. This app allows you to upload a video of any length or record it straight from the app. It then slices your video into 15 second portions you can upload to Instagram. Your followers will see one long, seamless video.

Phaze App:

Phaze is a great way to show your personality and build trust with future customers. Market your work on Instagram and Facebook, while building your portfolio with time-lapses and photo collages. Quickly capture project photos at each phase using our Edge-Ghost alignment tool to make perfect Time-Lapse Videos and Before/Mid/After Photo Collages. Then add selfie videos to explain what's changed since the last phase, what materials were used and what's coming next.

You can Instantly share videos as Instagram & Facebook Stories with our faster and smoother video generator that creates immersive no-cropping sweeping videos showing "What's Changed", revealing the process. Easily stay active on social, getting your brand and work in front of more users. Add your projects' web page as a 'swipe up' links to your stories, allowing users to fully experience your portfolio on the web. Create time-lapse videos with the client on camera, raving about your work generating the ultimate review. You can now pan across a project using the rear camera so you can show your work while narrating a specific project phase.

IGTV

A successful contracting Instagram profile obviously consists of curated, high-quality photos...but what about video? Is there a place for video in the contractor's Instagram marketing plan? Of course. A video can often convey a message and provide value in a way a photograph cannot.

If you're a contractor on IG looking for another way to provide value to your followers, IGTV gives you a way to do just that. It's simple, easy, and rewarding to be able to post videos of longer length on Instagram. Enjoy filming insight-rich and informational videos for your followers without even leaving the platform.

What is IGTV?

There are currently three ways to post videos on IG.

1.As an Instagram Post

2.On an Instagram Story

3.On Instagram TV (IGTV)

IGTV is Instagram's first ever long-form video platform. Where IG posts are limited to 60 seconds of video and IG stories are sliced up into 15 second increments, IGTV allows you to post videos up to an hour long.

The one limiting factor is that videos can only be posted in the vertical format, but that should not be a hindrance, since we've all grown accustomed to filming video for IG Stories.

Anyone with an Instagram account can start an IGTV channel, and the videos can be viewed either in IGTV's standalone app, or on the IGTV channel within the IG app.

Why Is IGTV Important?

The introduction of IGTV for the contractor's business account is exciting for several reasons. If you're wanting to post longer videos for your followers but haven't yet made the leap to open a YouTube channel, you can do that without even leaving the IG platform.

If most of what you post on your IG stories is long videos chopped up into 15 second portions, IGTV gives you a way to post those videos smoothly, leaving your IG stories for daily updates and before and after photos.

Be Yourself

You don't need a background in Hollywood to film successful videos for your IGTV channel! In fact, if your target audience is the regular homeowner, your marketing message actually has a lot more power when your videos are shot vulnerably and relatable. Your videos should cause your viewers to think, "this is a person just like me! If they can do this, so can I!"

I've seen quite a few contractors sharing vlog style videos where they start the IGTV video in their pickup and by the end are at a job site explaining something in detail. It's cut up and edited into a nice vlog style video, but it's in the vertical format. That's great use for IGTV—bringing your followers along with you on jobsites and explaining your work process.

Another great way to use the channel is instructional videos—film a series of how-to videos in the vertical format and post them (daily, weekly, monthly) on your IGTV channel to provide value to your followers.

Making Videos for IGTV

When you post your video to the IGTV channel you'll need to give your video a title and description. Include relevant keywords in the title and description so that IG users can find you when they're searching for videos related to your topic! You'll also need to select a cover photo for the video; it can be either the first frame of the video or any other frame from the video—whatever will make the most compelling cover and draw people to your video.

After your video is posted, interreact with other IG users in the comments as well as view statistical insights from your post in the "Insights" section.

CHAPTER 6

Expanding Your Contracting Company's Reach on Instagram

So, after you've made an Instagram account; after you've set up your business profile, posted your first good quality pictures of finished jobs; maybe even done a few Instagram stories showing the behind-scenes of your current project—What's the next step?

How do you take your initial number of followers, your first batch of interactions on social media and expand them into something larger and profitable for your business?

We're going to look at a few things you can do to expand your contracting company's reach on Instagram. Some of these steps are simple (geotagging your posts requires just a click of a button) while a few of them take more effort (networking with other contractors requires time and forethought), but each will be helpful to your end goal—using Instagram to grow your company!

Using Hashtags for Reach

Instagram hashtags (#hashtag) work within the app both as a search engine and a catalogue. Searching for specific hashtags within Instagram is the easiest way to find a localized and/or specific post. Searching for a hashtag on Instagram will show you all the posts on the app that contain that keyword.

It's been proven that Instagram posts with hashtags get much more interaction within the app than posts without hashtags. Without hashtags, it's easy for your posts to be seen once and then lost in the algorithm.

Hashtag all your posts with appropriate tags relating to your location, your project, and your company specifically. This makes your posts searchable by location, product, name, etc., and you are far more likely to get found on the app.

Include Your Location

Instagram is not *just* a photo-sharing platform, it also contains a very high-quality search engine. Instagram's search engine answers a user's search based on their location, past "likes," who they are following, etc.

One way to really take advantage of Instagram's search engine for the expansion of your company's Instagram account, is to always use the location feature. Posting pictures with your location allows any Instagram user (not just your followers!) to see your post when they search a certain location. If you've tagged your photos with your Seattle, WA location, every time Seattle, WA is searched, your photos will appear in the results.

Every time you post a picture of your work, make sure to enable your location settings and add your location to each post. I see a lot of people forget that, which is understandable, but remember how foundational your location is to your online presence. An Instagram user based in Canada won't be helped by your Phoenix, Arizona kitchen remodeling Instagram posts, but a fellow Phoenix resident looking to remodel their kitchen will be!

Research has shown that photos posted with a location get 79% more engagement than photos without a location. That's huge! If you want to be found by potential customers in your locality, you should always use your location when you post.

When you create an Instagram Story, add your location from the collection of stickers in the top right corner. Instagram creates a big story made of all the stories posted with that location, and Instagram users are automatically shown the featured stories from their city. Your story will be added to the collection of stories from your city, and anyone clicking on the featured story will see it!

Instagram rewards consistency.

There are two different types of consistency related to Instagram posts; one is consistency in the number of photos you post (one a day? One a week? Twice a day?); and the second is consistency in the content you post. We'll look at both of those types.

Consistency in Time/Amount of Posting

It's generally recognized that the more often you post on Instagram, the more opportunities there are for engagement with other Instagram users and more opportunities to be found within the app. That being said, 10+ photos a day could end up cluttering your follower's Instagram feeds and lead them to unfollow you. Moderation is important.

Decide for yourself and your company's brand, what works the best for you. Try posting once a day for a week and see what happens; try once a week. However, once you find what schedule/amount gives you the best interaction, stick with it consistently.

Consistency in Content

The most popular Instagram accounts maintain a cohesive 'theme' with each photo they post. Maybe it's the same filter applied to each photo, maybe they post inspirational quotes every three photos, maybe they always post before-and-after collages of their finished products.

You want your Instagram profile to look cohesive and tidy, not randomly cluttered or disorganized. Your followers come to expect a certain kind of post from you; that's why the follow you! They like your content. Try to reward them with consistency.

Networking with Other Contractors

Making connections is the key to growth on Instagram.

As soon as possible once you're active on Instagram, find your strategic partners and fellow contractors and connect with them on the app. Your strategic partners are people you work with in your town who don't directly compete with what you do. If you're a homebuilder, they're the landscape designers. If you're a plumber, maybe it's the home inspector. You want to connect with them and help them promote their companies on Instagram as well. Your fellow contractors, of course, are the men and women in the trenches with you. While you might often be competing for the same target audience, you can also help each other out by providing value and exposure to each other's companies on Instagram.

Post shout-outs about contractors you admire; share other contractor's work; like and comment on their posts; ask questions. Get to know the other contractors in your area by interacting with them on social media; this gives you more exposure every time your fellow contractor's followers come across your page or information.

Connect People to Your Website

We've established that Instagram is a great place to feature yourself and your work with show high quality images, but it's unlikely that you'll get all your business from an Instagram comment. If you're in the business of contracting, and you want to generate leads from your local market, what's the best way to do that?

People nowadays want to oversee their own research. They want to go online, research companies, and find who they specifically want to work for them. The best place for them to find out who you are and what you do, is your web site. It's your home base. All your social media, advertising, etc., should always point back to it. That way whenever people are searching for you online, they'll be directed to your website even if they found you on social media.

Link your website in the bio of your Instagram profile, direct potential customers to it often, whether you've posted a new blog post, are offering a sale, answering questions—anything. They can delve further into research there.

You might even want to form a web landing page specific to your business and link that in your Instagram bio. Design the page to answer your potential customer's questions. Tell them where they can get started. Click through to fill out a form with their contact information so you can follow up with them.

Make calls to action in the description of your posts or in your stories. There are many different ways to get potential customers to take action.

Finally, one thing you can do is sponsor your best performing posts within Instagram. If you want to pay a little bit to get in front of more people, go into your statistics and find some of your best performing posts; take one of your images that has done well and sponsor it for a week. If you spend a hundred dollars on something, choose your targeting wisely. You don't want the people seeing and liking your sponsored post to be only other contractors. You want to get it in front of as many potential customers and homeowners in your city as possible.

BONUS

Instagram Tips from Other Contractors

While putting this booklet together I reached out to a handful of contractors with a great Instagram presence to ask for their advice about Instagram.

Please take time to visit and follow each contractor's Instagram channel. Watch what they are doing. You will learn a ton just by watching these smart contractors do their thing on Instagram each and every day.

Kevin Ryffel

Real Renovations

@realrenovations

"As a small business owner, I find my work often speaks for itself. Using Instagram as my main source of marketing potential customers, to see what @realrenovations is truly capable of and the true beauty of our design. A few times a month, contractor lead companies like Networx, reach out to us, and try to persuade their marketing services.

Though through the years, @realrenovations has grown to over 50k followers, generating 3-5 quality leads a week. I find the most success in sharing quality posts. Our craftsmanship builds our following, saving us cost on marketing."

Austin King

Rafter House

@_rafterhouse_

"Our following on Instagram has helped tremendously in establishing our brand and following. It also continues to be one of our best social media platforms for lead generating the new clients needed to sustain and grow our business.

Over the years it has also helped to attract new sub-contractors, potential collaborations, and other promotional type opportunities that have been valuable to our brand. Each of these have been added benefits we initially did not intend to receive when we first created our Instagram account.

Building our following has taken several years of consistent and frequent posting, and intentional engagement with others to reach the where we're at. I've found there are no secrets to overnight success - just the steady and unwavering drive to continue posting good content with the end goal of building a loyal and engaged following."

Brad Leavitt

AFT Construction

@aft_construction

"We have been asked many times about our growth and following on Instagram. The key to our success is engagement. We have built a "niche" following in our market because of our resolution to respond to customer's questions and inquiries. Not only do we respond to questions and direct messages, but we also engage on other accounts. We have built a vast network of builders, designers, and contractors all throughout the country. This has enabled us to network, share industry pricing, techniques and marketing strategies.

We have also built our following but engaging with many individual personal users. We target certain cities, hashtags, and events in the Phoenix area. We like pictures and engage with those who live in our demographic. In turn, many of them follow and engage with our account. There is no doubt that this is a large time commitment, however, the reward is grand. We have received numerous leads that have converted into actual projects of substantial value.

When you have a spokesperson behind your company willing to engage and comment, people will see the genuine effort and respond."

Kyle Stumpenhorst

Rural Renovators

@rrbuilders

"Instagram stories play a huge role in connecting with your audience it gives them a chance to see who you really are and what type of person is behind those awesome pictures they see on their daily feed. By being real and opening yourself up to transparency whether that is your business your life your family. It gives your followers the opportunity to connect with you. once the connection has been made and they feel like they can talk to you, interact with you, and relate to you they are even more apt to engage and help your feed grow."

Jamie & Morgan Molitor

Construction2Style Renovators

@construction2style

"The world is changing and FAST. Social Media has changed the way people connect with one another and simply live their lives. You can get your business in front of millions of people within minutes now online and Instagram is one of the best places to do just that. Instagram is the only social platform where people follow someone for intent, a specific reason. Yes, you may not want clients in another state but if they start talking about you, you never know who knows who and where and what that will lead to.

By sharing photos of your work, the most important thing you are doing is building a relationship. Then you're building trust and showcasing just how darn talented you are. Share photos of not only your work but your lifestyle, team, family. This will also show that you are human and in turn will lead to a better working relationship with your potential new clients. They will remember that you are a father, mother, son, daughter, brother, sister and will talk to you that way. My biggest advice when it comes to the Instagram game is to give, give, give, give, give a little more, and then ask for that business. When you do that, they'll all show up and give it to you."

MORE BOOKS IN THIS SERIES:

Get a FREE Copy at
ContractorMarketingSimplified.com

(S&H required. Offer valid in the USA Only)

ABOUT THE AUTHOR

Martin Holsinger is a #1 Amazon Bestselling author, speaker, and contractor marketing expert. His experience as a residential contractor gives him inside knowledge into an industry few other marketers understand. He primarily focuses on helping contractors build their online presence and get found by their ideal customers.